Book 8

God's Team

By Rick Tancreto
Art by Mary Bausman

Piney Point, Maryland

www.LittleSaintsPress.com

Dedication

For my children,
Rick and Diane,
and their precious families.
—Pops

With thanks to my mother and dad, my husband, Cal, and my dear family
for continuing to put crayons in my hands.
And a special thanks to God for guiding each creative stroke.
—M.B.

Unless otherwise noted, all Bible texts are from the Holy Bible, New Living Translation, copyright © 1996, 2004, 2007 by Tyndale House Foundation. Used by permission of Tyndale House Publishers, Inc., Carol Stream, Illinois 60188. All rights reserved.

Bible texts credited to CEV are from the Contemporary English Version®. Copyright © 1995 American Bible Society. All rights reserved. Bible text from the Contemporary English Version (CEV) is not to be reproduced in copies or otherwise by any means except as permitted in writing by American Bible Society, 1865 Broadway, New York, NY 10023 (www.americanbible.org).

Scriptures credited to ERV are from the Easy-to-Read Version. Copyright © 2006 World Bible Translation Center.

Bible texts marked GNT are from the Good News Translation® (Today's English Version, Second Edition) Copyright © 1992 American Bible Society. All rights reserved.

Scripture credited to GW is taken from GOD'S WORD®, © 1995 God's Word to the Nations. Used by permission of Baker Publishing Group.

Scriptures credited to NCV are from the New Century Version. Copyright © 2005 by Thomas Nelson, Inc. Used by permission. All rights reserved.

Scripture marked NKJV are taken from the New King James Version®. Copyright © 1982 by Thomas Nelson, Inc. Used by permission. All rights reserved.

Bible texts credited to NIV are taken from the Holy Bible, New International Version®, NIV® Copyright © 1973, 1978, 1984, 2011 by Biblica, Inc.® Used by permission. All rights reserved worldwide.

Scriptures marked NIrV are taken from the Holy Bible, New International Reader's Version®. Copyright © 1996, 1998 Biblica. All rights reserved throughout the world. Used by permission of Biblica.

Scriptures credited to NLV are from the New Life Version, © Christian Literature International.

Verses marked TLB are taken from The Living Bible, copyright © 1971 by Tyndale House Publishers, Wheaton, Ill. Used by permission.

Printed in the United States by BOOKMASTERS, 30 Amberwood Parkway, Ashland OH 44805

Job No.: 50005825
Production Date: August, 2014

This book was written by Rick Tancreto (Rick@LittleSaintsPress.com); edited by Lori Peckham; designed by square1studio; illustrated by Mary Bausman © 2014 (www.marybausman.com).
Children Advisers: Karalyn & Nicholas Ashenfelter; Dominick & Danny Caparotti; Cara Driscoll; Reef Peckham; Connor, Ellie, Luke, Joy, Lucy, & Malachi Senechal.

Tancreto, Rick.
God's team / by Rick Tancreto ; art by Mary Bausman.
pages cm — (Hang on to Jesus! adventures ; book 8)
SUMMARY: When Ricky and Dee Dee set sail for distant shores in their almost-a-boat float, Jesus helps them discover how to be a really good team player—on God's team.
Audience: Ages 6-12.
LCCN 2 0 1 2 9 2 3 9 4 3
ISBN 978-1-936831-08-1

1. Jesus Christ—Juvenile fiction. 2. Church—
Juvenile fiction. 3. Christian life—Juvenile fiction.
[1. Jesus Christ—Fiction. 2. Church—Fiction.
3. Christian life—Fiction.] I. Bausman, Mary,
illustrator. II. Title. III. Series: Tancreto, Rick.
Hang on to Jesus! adventures ; bk. 8.

PZ7.T161355Goe 2014   [E]
QBI14-600114

"Do everything in love."

1 Corinthians 16:14 (NIV)

Dee Dee brushed some strands of hair from her face and sighed. "I'm tired of building this float," she announced.

"Yeah, it's getting boring," Ricky agreed, wiping his sweaty hands on his pants.

The children had spent most of that summer morning cutting, taping, and decorating a float. Their baseball team, the Little Saints, needed one for the county fair parade, and they'd volunteered to build it.

Dee Dee stood back and wondered out loud, "What if our float wins first place? How **gratifying** would *that* be!"

Ricky stopped his work on the sail and commented, "That'd be pretty cool . . . since we already know what it's like to finish in *last* place!"

"Just because we didn't win as many games as we wanted to doesn't mean we're not a good team," Dee Dee defended. "And it doesn't mean our float can't win the first-place ribbon."

Ricky pointed to his uniform. "We didn't win even half of our games this season. Anyway, who cares? What I want to do is see if we can get our float to *float*. Do you think it can—on the water, I mean?"

Dee Dee squinted her eyes. "It'll sink like a rock."

Ricky tried once more to convince his sister that their float was seaworthy. "Look, when we get it in the water, I'll be the captain and you can be my first mate."

"You mean *I'll* be the captain!" Dee Dee asserted.

"Come on," Ricky said impatiently. "Help me get it down to the dock so we can try it out."

Dee Dee crossed her arms. "I'm not getting in that thing. Our float won't float!"

Just then the children heard a familiar voice: "I can make it float."

Dee Dee's mouth fell open. "Ricky! Jesus has come to visit us again!" She raced into His arms, with her brother close behind.

"Hi, children," said Jesus as He hugged each of them. Then He circled their float and looked over their creation. "I know how hard you've worked on this," He said with a smile.

The children stood in silence, waiting to hear what their Savior would say next. "Yes," He proclaimed, "*this* is the float that will win first place at the county fair."

The children continued to stand in silence. They couldn't believe their ears. Finally, Ricky managed to gasp: "We did it? We're going to win?"

"That's right," answered Jesus.

Ricky immediately raised his hand and gave a vigorous high-five to Jesus, then to

"I consider everything to be nothing compared to knowing Christ Jesus

Dee Dee. Next, Dee Dee gave a high-five to Jesus and then one back to her brother. Maxie just watched with her tongue dangling out of her mouth.

"It doesn't get any better than this!" exclaimed Ricky.

"Well," Jesus said kiddingly, "I guess that means you wouldn't want to go on another adventure with Me."

"Oh, yes we would!" blurted out Dee Dee. "That'd be *way* better than winning a **paltry** ribbon, right, Ricky?"

"Of course! Of course, it would!" Ricky quickly agreed, trying to erase his earlier statement.

"OK," Jesus said with a laugh. "We'll use your float for our adventure. Go get your sailing gear, and I'll meet you down at the dock."

my Lord. To know him is the best thing of all." Philippians 3:8 (NIrV)

Soon the children darted off the front porch and raced each other to the dock.

"Hey, Dee Dee," panted Ricky, "did you remember to bring your life vest?"

"Yup," answered Dee Dee. "It's in my backpack with my Bible."

What's she doing bringing her Bible? Ricky thought to himself.

As they arrived dockside, Jesus was waiting for them—and so was their float.

"You made it float, Lord!" applauded Dee Dee.

Ricky bolted to the edge of the dock, his eyes almost as large as his compass. "Lord, our float is . . . afloat. It's now a boat!"

Jesus smiled at them and said, "If you're ready, let's go aboard."

Reaching into his pocket, Ricky looked at Jesus. "I brought my compass to help us navigate to unknown lands and distant shores. Hey, that reminds me, Lord, where are You taking us?"

"Brothers and sisters, God loves you. And we know that he

As Jesus untied the boat from the dock, He answered, "On a journey to see My church."

"Great!" responded Dee Dee. "And once we've visited Your church, we can show You ours. So . . . are we ready to shove off, Lord?"

"We're ready."

As the children hoisted up the sail, Jesus began to explain, "When I said we would see My church, I wasn't referring to a building. By itself, a building isn't the church. The church is made up of people I call My brothers and sisters."

"Does that mean that all of the people in Your church are *related*?" asked Ricky.

"Yes," replied Jesus. "Even though they have different skin colors and speak different languages and come from different countries around the world, they're all bound together as one large family."

"That would be God's family, right, Jesus?" confirmed Dee Dee.

"Yes, and you're all in God's family because—"

"Because each of us believes in You, Lord!" Ricky finished Jesus' sentence.

"Exactly. You're all brothers and sisters in the family of God because you believe in Me. And *that's* My church!"

has chosen you to be his people." 1 Thessalonians 1:4 (ERV)

"The church became stronger, as the Holy Spirit

As a slight breeze filled the sail, the boat drifted away from the dock.

"We're off!" shouted Ricky enthusiastically. "All hands on deck! We're sailing to far-off distant shores to discover Jesus' church! Lord, *You* be our captain, and Dee Dee, you can be—"

Dee Dee turned toward the bow and interrupted her brother: "Ricky, we've just started our journey—do you think you could *calm down*?" She turned back around and asked Jesus to tell her more about His church.

"It's kind of like your boat," He said.

"Really?" Dee Dee asked. "How so, Lord?"

Jesus reached down and put His hand in the water. "The Holy Spirit is a lot like the wind that fills the sail of your boat. He uses His power to fill My church, helping to move it along as it grows and becomes stronger."

Ricky looked up into the sky and then back down at the sail. "The Holy Spirit is *everywhere*! Evv-ree-where!"

Dee Dee cleared her throat loudly. Ricky recognized this as his signal to stop repeating, "The Holy Spirit is *everywhere*!"

Grinning, Ricky pretended to hide his face behind his compass. This gave Dee Dee an idea for her next question: "Lord, does Your church have a compass?"

"Yes, but it's a spiritual compass. It always points in the same direction—toward Me."

Ricky peered down at his compass. *I wish mine were a spiritual compass*, he thought to himself. "What about a manual, Lord?" he asked. "Every well-equipped boat has a manual that helps the crew find their way and keep on course. Is there such a thing as a manual for Your church?"

Jesus directed the children's eyes to the Bible in Dee Dee's lap. "That's our manual for My church."

Dee Dee smiled and gripped her Bible a little tighter.

encouraged it and helped it grow." Acts 9:31 (CEV)

8

"Wheee!" squealed Dee Dee as the boat lifted up on a wave and then slid down. "This is so fun!"

Ricky was also having a grand time, especially since he no longer carried the responsibility of being the captain. "Boats have captains," he reflected, "and my baseball team has a captain. So, is there a captain of Your church, Lord?"

"Yes," Jesus revealed. "God the Father gave Me authority over everything on earth and in heaven, including My church."

"So it truly is *Your* church!" Dee Dee pointed out.

"I'm the head of the church," acknowledged Jesus, "and because I love you and everyone else in it, I died on the cross. Now I pray to God the Father for all of My brothers and sisters, using each of your names."

"For real?" Ricky said in a wheezy voice.

"Yes, and when the time comes, I'll introduce you to your Father in heaven."

Wide-eyed, the children looked at each other. *A personal introduction to God the Father by His Son when we enter heaven!* they thought excitedly.

"We will speak the truth in love, growing in every way more and more

like Christ, who is the head of his body, the church." Ephesians 4:15

By this time Jesus and the children had sailed to the end of the channel and were moving into unfamiliar waters.

"Looks like nothing but blue skies and calm seas ahead," Ricky observed as he trimmed the sail.

Dee Dee busied herself putting her backpack and Bible under the seat. "Everything on board is **shipshape** for our adventure," she reported. "The three of us make a *gooood* team."

As Ricky finished lashing down the sail, he pointed to it: "Yeah, sis, just like our baseball team."

Dee Dee scrunched up her nose. "Huh?"

"Little Saints," said Ricky, pointing again to the sail. "Even though we finished in last place, we still played well together because all of us depended on one another to do our part. You know, Dee Dee, we can't have nine players out there doing their own thing!"

"Everybody knows *that*," Dee Dee responded as she squinted her eyes and wrinkled her brow.

"And we're *gooood*," needled Ricky, "because each of us plays the position we were made

"Just as there are many parts to our bodies, so it is with Christ's body. We are all have different work to do. So we belong to each

for. You cover second base, and I'm the shortstop, and Maxie is the mascot, and Reef is the catcher, and Ron—"

"Yeah, he's our left fielder," cut in Dee Dee. "I get it. But what I really want to know is what are our positions on board this *boat*?"

"That's easy," Ricky jumped in. "Jesus is the captain, I'm first mate, and you're the deckhand."

"No way!" Dee Dee gave a double thumbs-down to her brother's idea.

"*Yes* way!" teased Ricky. "What do You say, Lord . . . sound like a *gooood* team to You?"

Jesus smiled at both of them. "You know, you're also on another good team—a team in which everyone is equally important to the success of the team, no matter what position they play."

"The only other team I can think of is my soccer team," responded Ricky.

"Your soccer team is a good team, but I'm talking about the greatest team of all. On this team everyone is called to be a saint."

"A little saint . . . like our baseball team?" Ricky inquired.

"No, Ricky, He's talking about the church, right, Jesus?" Dee Dee said. "That's *got* to be the greatest team of all."

"Yes, just like the Little Saints, the church works as one team, with each person dependent on the others."

"Does everyone in the church have a position that they were made for, Lord?" asked Ricky.

"Yes, and when you find your special position in the church, you can then use your talents to serve others."

The children nodded in agreement. "Hey," Ricky concluded, "we're on two saint teams— our baseball team *and* the church team!"

parts of it, and it takes every one of us to make it complete, for we each other, and each needs all the others." Romans 12:4, 5 (TLB)

"Now that we're underway, how would each of you like a turn at sailing the boat?" offered Jesus.

"Me first! Me first!" claimed Ricky. "I called it!"

Ricky tried to stand up and take his position at the tiller, but his efforts were thwarted by his sister holding him in his seat.

"Lord, do I bear any **resemblance** to my brothers and sisters in the family of God?" asked Dee Dee.

"Well," said Jesus, "you don't necessarily look like one another."

Trying to move the conversation along so he could steer the boat, Ricky interjected: "That's because we're all from different countries, have different skin colors, and speak different languages. Now, *that* should answer all your questions, sis." Ricky stood up.

"Ricky's right," said Jesus. "And yet those in My church are alike in many ways."

"Lord," implored Dee Dee, "please teach us how we're all alike."

"Oh," sighed Ricky deeply. "I'll never get to steer." He sat back down.

Putting His hand on Ricky's shoulder, Jesus spoke: "The most important similarity of all is that we're bound together by love."

Ricky muttered, "You don't mean the kissin' kind of love, do You, Lord?"

"I mean the Godly kind of love. Do you recall seeing Me with a washbasin and towel?"

"Sure do. You washed the feet of Your disciples to show how we too should serve each other."

"Right," said Jesus. "That's the kind of love we should show one another—serving others and expecting nothing in return."

"Putting others first," added Dee Dee, "even before ourselves."

"Yes," smiled Jesus, "and putting God before all others."

"That's awfully hard to do," admitted Dee Dee as she shuffled her feet. "I think we're all a little selfish."

"That may be true, but when you love in a Godly way, you'll discover the great joy it brings—not only to God and others, but to yourself as well."

"I've got a great idea!" announced Ricky as he stood up and nearly fell out of the boat. "Jesus, You said that love brings great joy to everyone. Well, the 'j' in the word joy could stand for 'Jesus'; the 'o' could stand for 'others'; and the 'y' could stand for 'yourself.' *J.O.Y.!*"

"That's the **priority** of how we should love!" Dee Dee figured out. "Jesus is first above all others, then comes everyone else, and then me."

"Jesus answered: Love the Lord your God with all your heart, soul, and mind. This commandment is like this one. And it is, 'Love others

"Works for me!" agreed Ricky.

"Works for Me," agreed Jesus.

Ricky was now ready to take his turn sailing the boat. But as he stood up, he silently questioned himself: *If I take my turn before my sister, I'll be spelling "J.O.Y." more like "J.Y.O." H'mmm.* "Hey, Dee Dee, you take the helm first," he offered.

Dee Dee jumped to her feet and quickly moved toward the stern. "Thanks!"

Jesus smiled over at Ricky.

is the first and most important commandment. The second most important as much as you love yourself.'" Matthew 22:37-39 (CEV)

A strong tailwind pushed the boat toward the open sea, much to Ricky's delight. He adjusted the sail to make it to go even faster, and they began to skim across the water. "Now we're motoring!" he shouted.

"You mean *sailing*, not motoring," corrected Dee Dee. "You need a motor to be motoring, and you need a sail to be sailing, and we have a sail and not a motor, so—"

"Enough already!" Ricky flopped down on the seat. "I get it."

"Let love make you serve one

"*Gooood*," ribbed Dee Dee. "Now maybe we can get back to the important stuff." She scratched her head thoughtfully and turned toward Jesus. "Lord, would You teach us how to express our love for You in real ways?"

"And for *others*," added Ricky, glaring at his sister.

Jesus put His arms around both of them. "Sure," He said. "The Holy Spirit set you apart for God's service. This means your love is reflected through your works of service." Jesus directed the children to look down into the water.

"Hey, I can see our **reflections**!" noted Dee Dee. "I see You, Jesus, and you, Ricky."

"And those you see are those you serve. You serve Me first, then others, and then yourself."

"Hey, Ricky, Jesus just used your J.O.Y.!" recounted Dee Dee. "That's pretty awesome."

Ricky's glare melted away. Looking up at Jesus, he asked, "But what do we have that we can use to serve You and others?"

"God has equipped you with all you need to perform works of service," said Jesus. "You can use your time, your talents, and your treasure."

"Ohhh, Dee Dee," teased Ricky, "I've got another great idea! Let me see . . . time . . . talents . . . treasure. They all begin with the letter 't'. I guess that makes them the 3 T's!"

"OK, Ricky," cried Dee Dee, "enough with the **acronyms**!"

"With *what*?" Ricky looked confused.

"You know," Dee Dee said, "like BFF stands for Best Friends Forever. You did the same thing with your 3 T's—they stand for Time, Talents, Treasure."

"Thanks, sis." Ricky grinned. "*Now* I'll put you back on my list of BFFs!"

Laughter filled the boat.

Still smiling, Jesus added, "Remember, when you show your love for Me and others through your service, you shouldn't expect recognition or praise or rewards for your actions. To do so would mean you didn't serve out of Godly love, but out of a desire to be given credit for what you did."

"Then it's impossible to serve others with Godly love," summarized Dee Dee, "if your love is self-serving."

Jesus nodded.

A series of huge waves crashed against the hull. "Dee Dee," Ricky yelled, "we need to batten down the hatches! We're entering rough seas."

"Uh, Ricky," said Dee Dee with a puzzled look on her face, "there are no hatches to batten down."

"Um, well then, you need to *sit* down. We're entering rough seas."

"OK, Ricky, consider it done." Dee Dee sat down, wanting to continue her conversation with Jesus anyway. "Lord, I know I can find the time to serve, and I can even

"Let love be your highest goal! But you should also desire

find some treasure from my allowance to give to others. But what talents do I have to serve with? Can I serve my teammates with my talent of playing second base?"

"Sure you can. But I'm talking about *spiritual* talents that are revealed to you by the Holy Spirit. Your spiritual talent might be showing kindness to people, or sharing the Good News about Me, or giving generously of your money to others, or teaching a friend about Me, or serving at your church. Whatever your talent is, it comes from above. It's a spiritual *gift* to you."

"It's a *spiritual* gift because it comes from the Holy *Spirit*, right, Jesus?" asked Dee Dee.

"Yes, and with these gifts you can serve your brothers and sisters in My church."

I gotta admit it, Dee Dee thought to herself. *Ricky was right when he said that the Holy Spirit is everywhere!*

the special abilities the Spirit gives." 1 Corinthians 14:1

The sun began to set, casting the water and sky in brilliant colors.

"Lord," said Dee Dee, "please teach us how else Ricky and I resemble our brothers and sisters in Your church."

"I'll give you a hint. It has something to do with what you brought on board."

Dee Dee's eyes scoured the boat. "My Bible!"

"That's right," said Jesus. "My church has a desire to not only read Scripture and obey its teachings, but to be changed by it."

"*Changed?*" repeated Ricky. "How so, Lord?"

"Do what God's teaching says; when you only listen sand do nothing, you are fooling yourselves." James 1:22 (NCV)

"Do you recall seeing Jeremiah the prophet?"

"Oh, yes," answered Dee Dee. "We got to watch the Holy Spirit breathe into him to bring God's Word to life."

Jesus nodded. "God's Word is alive, and when you read it and obey My teachings, it'll become active in your lives by guiding your thoughts, words, and actions."

This was almost more than the children could grasp.

"I can't think of any other book that's so powerful," Dee Dee said.

Jesus smiled. "It's through the power of the Holy Spirit that God's Word is changing you—to be more and more like Me."

"Did you hear that, Dee Dee?" questioned Ricky. "How many times have I said that the Holy Spirit is *everywhere*?"

"How about *toooo* many?"

Laughter again filled the boat.

"God's word is living and active." Hebrews 4:12 (GW)

Ricky was feeling kind of brave now that he was sure he'd mastered the skill of seamanship. "Let's go really, really far," he said boldly. "Let's sail to distant lands!"

"OK," agreed Jesus, "but be ready to hold on."

As they prepared the boat for the long voyage that awaited them, Dee Dee thought about a conversation she'd had with Lori, her best friend: *Lori once told me that she doesn't need heaven or Jesus. That might mean she's not part of His church. But I am. Now what do I do? Can I still be her friend?*

"Lord," Dee Dee asked, "should we hang out with only people who are in Your church?"

"You are to love everyone, including Lori. God wants you to use your time, talents, and treasure to help spread the Good News to all who haven't received it."

As Jesus finished speaking, the boat began to bob up and down and move from side to side. It had sailed into waters unlike anything the children had ever seen from their dock. Frantically they looked aft and forward. All they could see were rough waters surrounding them.

"Where are we?" pleaded Ricky. He looked off into the distance and could barely make out the gloomy islands that dotted the horizon. "Jesus, we've traveled *too* far! We're in a place that can't be part of Your church."

"That's right," said Jesus calmly. "But this place is still the responsibility of My church. Imagine that there are people on those islands. Imagine that the ship they were sailing on wrecked and they were washed up on the beach. They're now stranded and separated from the mainland and from all other people."

"They're like **castaways**," Dee Dee thought aloud. "They're lost and need to be rescued."

"And the same is true for people who aren't part of My church," said Jesus. "They too are lost because they're separated from God. They need rescuing."

"That's why You died on the cross, Lord," said Ricky. "To rescue us from our sin and eternal separation from God."

"Well said, Ricky. You know and believe that, and now you're equipped to share the Good News about Me with those who may not trust in Me."

"For the Son of Man came to look for and to save from the

"Then they could become our brothers and sisters in Your church, Jesus—and no longer lost!" hoped Dee Dee.

Jesus nodded. "And remember, when you talk with your friends about Me, always be gentle and respectful. They may not understand or accept everything you want to tell them. That's OK. Allow the Holy Spirit to do His work in their hearts."

Hearing the mention of the Holy Spirit, Ricky immediately glanced over at his sister, cocked his head, and grinned.

"Don't you dare say 'The Holy Spirit is *everywhere*,'" warned Dee Dee.

Ricky kept silent—but he did pat himself on the back, twice.

punishment of sin those who are lost." Luke 19:10 (NLV)

"Children," said Jesus, "it's time to head home."

Reluctantly, Dee Dee moved to the stern and pushed the tiller as far as it would go to starboard. The boat began to drift in the direction of home. As the waves lapped up against the bow, Dee Dee turned to Jesus and asked: "Lord, how else do we resemble our brothers and sisters?"

"The saints in My church consider it important to be in worship of God."

Ricky's ears perked up. He thought he heard Jesus say "warship." "*I'm* up for turning our boat into God's warship!"

"Oh, brother!" cried Dee Dee, smacking her forehead with her hand. "Jesus didn't say *warship*—He said **worship**."

"Ahhh," squeaked Ricky, his voice trailing off. "Never mind."

"You worship God whenever you give Him honor and respect," explained Jesus.

"Like when we're at church and we sing to Him," stated Ricky.

"Yes," said Jesus, "and He wants you to make worship part of everything you do."

"Then, Lord," requested Ricky, "please teach us how we can worship Him throughout the entire day."

"You can *serve* Him all day long."

"Serve *God?*" Ricky's face was all scrunched up.

"Sure," said Jesus. "You're serving Him whenever you use your 3 T's to serve others."

Wow, Jesus just used my acronym for time, talents, and treasure, Ricky realized. *Pretty cool!*

"You also worship Him by loving Him," said Jesus.

"There's our word again," blared out Dee Dee. "Love!"

"And another way to worship God," continued Jesus, "is to enjoy your personal relationship with Him."

"But Lord, I never quite understood how we do that," admitted Dee Dee.

"Help me make worshiping your name the most

"Well, what's the first thing you need in order to have a good relationship with somebody?" asked Jesus.

Dee Dee struggled with this question. Then the answer was right there in front of her. "Good **communication**! Just like we have with You, Lord."

"That's it!" responded Jesus. "You can communicate with God through your prayers and by giving Him praise and thanks. And He speaks to you through His Word as it's brought to life for you by the Holy Spirit."

Ricky stood up, opened his mouth wide, and was about to speak—until his sister cleared her throat. "Never mind," said Ricky. He sat back down.

important thing in my life." Psalm 86:11 (ERV)

"Glory belongs to God in the church and in Christ Jesus

Approaching the dock, Dee Dee barked out orders, as if she were now the captain: "Ricky, **stow** all of your gear for docking and **furl** the sail so it doesn't flap in the breeze."

"Ugh," recoiled Ricky. He began to think of a sarcastic response to his sister's unfair demands: *The only things flapping in the breeze are your lips! Yeah, that's a good one!* But thinking about the real meaning of love, Ricky kept his words to himself and went about his assigned duties.

Jesus smiled at Ricky.

As they landed dockside, Dee Dee secured the lines and promptly announced: "Prepare to **disembark**!"

"This adventure, Lord, has been way better than winning a ribbon," shared Ricky as he stepped off the boat. "I really wish it could go on forever."

Jesus took Ricky's hand. "Even though our adventure is coming to an end, My church will never end. Someday, you'll all gather together in heaven and live with Me for eternity."

"You've taken us on another adventure that begins here on earth and continues right into heaven!" Dee Dee rejoiced.

"Hey, speaking of heaven," added Ricky, "do You think we could bring our boat with us?"

Jesus smiled.

for all time and eternity! Amen." Ephesians 3:21 (GW)

Flap . . . flap . . . flap . . .

The wind whipped through the unfurled sail, startling both children out of their unplanned nap.

"What's this?" Dee Dee said as she noticed that the paint had dried on her paintbrush in the hot August sun. "Ricky, you fell asleep on the job and now you've ruined our brush."

"Then fire me," snapped Ricky. He stretched and yawned. "Anyway, I'm *done* with this painting thing. I'm going down to the dock to cool off."

"Wait a minute!" Dee Dee said as she thought about her brother's comment. "Didn't we just have a dream about going on an adventure with Jesus in our float?"

"Hey, we did!" recalled Ricky. "He taught us all about His church and—"

"Ricky, Dee Dee, time to come in and take your showers," a voice from the porch called out. "We have church tomorrow."

Ricky scrambled to his feet. "Let's go."

Dee Dee called, "I'm first in the shower!"

"Jesus taught us all about His church," Ricky remembered as he ran toward the house. "It's all about living out our Christian faith. Oh yeah, and doing *everything* with love!"

As the children threw open the door, Dee Dee stopped and turned toward her brother. "You think our float will win the first-place ribbon, like Jesus said?"

"I *know* so," Ricky said confidently as the door slammed behind him. "He always keeps His promises."

Dee Dee smiled. "You can shower first, Ricky."

YOUR
TURN ▶

Being on Jesus' team sounds wonderful!
How do I join His team?

Have you ever heard your named called to join a team? The captain and the members of the team wanted you to be one of their teammates! How awesome that must have made you feel.

Jesus is also calling your name. He wants to have you on His team—the greatest team of all. And when you become a team member, He has a special position for you to play.

So how do you join Jesus' team? By putting your trust in the Captain of the team! Jesus

came down from heaven to rescue us from our sin . . . the same sin that separates us from God. He did for us what we couldn't do for ourselves— He died on a cross to pay the penalty for our sin. And He did something else amazing. He rose from the grave and went back up to heaven. So now any person who believes in what Jesus did for them will go to heaven too!

"God showed his great love for us by sending Christ to die for us while we were still sinners." Romans 5:8

Do you believe that Jesus died for you? If so, then God the Father invites you to pray to Him:

Dear Father in heaven,

I want to join Jesus' team. On that team He's the Captain, and I'm called to be a saint.

I know that I'm a sinner and on my own I can't get on His team.

I believe that Jesus died on the cross to pay the penalty for my sins.

Please forgive me for all of my thoughts, words, and actions that go against Your character.

I believe that Jesus rose from the dead so that I would no longer be separated from You.

Thank You, Father, for sending Your Son—the Captain of my team—to rescue me.

Amen.

If you prayed this prayer and believed what you said, you can be certain that you're now a member of Jesus' team! And someday He'll welcome you to your new eternal home, heaven, where you'll meet all your teammates—and the team Captain!

"You are no longer strangers and foreigners, but fellow citizens with the saints and members of the household of God." Ephesians 2:19 (NKJV)